The Legendary Hunters of Texas

A True story of Honor, Courage and Commitment

By Paul "Pauly" Freeman

THE LEGENDARY HUNTERS OF TEXAS

A TRUE STORY OF HONOR, COURAGE AND COMMITMENT

BY PAUL "PAULY" FREEMAN

PUBLISHING BY

SELF PUBLISHED

DEDICATED

TO THE MEN AND WOMEN OF VF-201 AND VFA-201 HUNTERS

"ONCE A HUNTER ALWAYS A HUNTER"

Special appreciation to my fellow Hunters for their support in providing me with ideas to get the book accomplished. I could not have written this book without all their support.

Hunters can still make a difference. All proceeds from the book sales will be donated back to the Veterans 22Kill Program and the Gary Sinise Foundation which raises awareness to veteran suicide and mental health issues such as Post Traumatic Stress Disorder (PTSD) to our veterans that an average of 22 veterans are committing suicide daily.

THE LEGENDARY HUNTERS OF TEXAS

A TRUE STORY OF HONOR, COURAGE AND COMMITMENT

ALL RIGHTS RESERVED

NO PART OF THIS DOCUMENT MAY BE COPIED OR REPRODUCED IN ANY WAY WITHOUT THE EXPRESS PERMISSION OF THE AUTHOR

ALL PHOTOGRAPHY IN THIS BOOK COMES FROM SOCIAL MEDIA POSTS FROM FELLOW HUNTER SQUADRON MEMBERS

SELF PUBLISHED, 2016

Copyright © 2016 Paul "Pauly" Freeman
ISBN: 1537538055
ISBN 13: 9781537538051
Library of Congress Control Number: **XXXXX (If applicable)**
LCCN Imprint Name: **City and State (If applicable)**

PRINTING COORDINATED BY

LIMITED FIRST EDITION

COVER PHOTO – VFA-201 F-18

BACK COVER

"It is not the critic who counts; not the man who points out how the strong man stumbles, or where the doer of deeds could have done them better. The credit belongs to the man who is actually in the arena, whose face is marred by dust and sweat and blood; who strives valiantly; who errs, who comes short again and again, because there is no effort without error and shortcoming; but who does actually strive to do the deeds; who knows great enthusiasms, the great devotions; who spends himself in a worthy cause; who at the best knows in the end the triumph of high achievement, and who at the worst, if he fails, at least fails while daring greatly, so that his place shall never be with those cold and timid souls who neither know victory nor defeat".

- Theodore Roosevelt

CONTENTS

WHY WRITE A BOOK ABOUT THIS SQUADRON	9
THE BEGINNING	12
F-4 DAYS	19
F-14 DAYS	24
F-18 DAYS	38
RESERVISTS CALLED TO WAR	44
UNDERWAY	49
OIF OPERATIONS	53
HOMECOMING	64
HUNTERS INTO THE SUNSET – DECOMMISIONING	68
HUNTERS ROSTER OIF SHOCK AND AWE MISSIONS	72
HUNTERS ACHIEVE EXCELLENCE	75
WHAT IS A VETERAN	79
ABOUT THE AUTHOR	81

WHY WRITE A BOOK ABOUT THIS SQUADRON

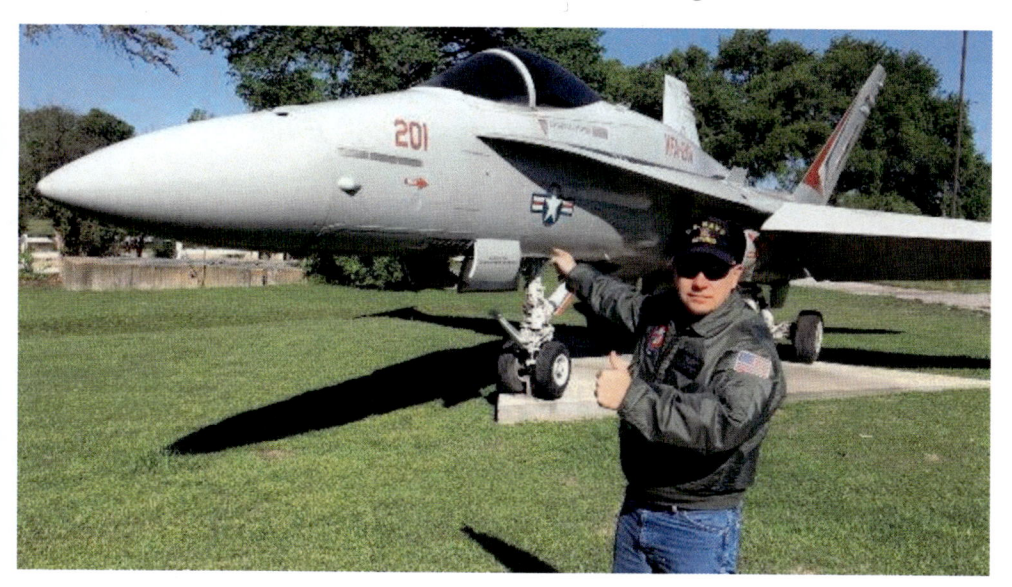

I spent my last seven years of my 20 year Naval career serving in the squadron during both F-14 and F-18 eras. For me the desire to capture our squadrons' great history hit me like a ton of bricks recently when I went to the old base at NAS JRB Fort Worth for a visit. Anyways, as I pulled up to the front gate one Saturday afternoon I saw our static display F-18. With excitement, I asked my wife if she would be so kind to get a picture of me standing beside our old jet. The picture above is that picture my wife had taken. As we proceeded through the front gate security of the base I saw our F-14 on static display and smiled. I then wanted to go see our old hangar and as we approached the hangar, I saw that the painting on the outside of our hangar had been erased. As most veterans do we reflect on our service to our country and the folks we served with. As I sat outside our old hangar, I had a rush of emotions thinking that our squadron had literally been forgotten. I felt impelled to get on social media and share those feelings with my fellow Hunters. I mentioned that our squadron has been forgotten and that someone needs to write a book. To my surprise many social media Hunters chimed in and said I should write a book. Well I was a little taken back from the response and thought to myself, can I make this happen, and after all just like everyone else these days we are all very busy.

So, the question of why would I write a book about the VF-201 / VFA-201 Hunter Squadron is an easy one for me. The Hunter squadron of Texas has been forgotten. Of course, there are the social media mechanisms that are flooded with our squadrons' great history but there is no single document that I can find that captures our full history in detail.

My goal for this book is twofold. One write a simple book that captures our basic history all in one document and two is to attempt to sell the book and donate all the sales from the book back to a Veterans Program to bring awareness that many of our Veterans today are committing suicide and struggling with life during their post military service days. The photos and the information in this book have all been gathered from social media sights or have been provided from fellow Hunters. By no means did I write this book to bring attention to myself nor make anyone else upset because they may have been left out of the book.

11

THE BEGINNING

VF-201 F8H Aircraft

The United States Naval Reserve fighter squadron VF-201, The Hunters, was commissioned in July 1970 as part of Carrier Air Wing Twenty (CVWR-20) during the reorganization of the Naval Reserve Force. The result was a fully operational fighting force consisting of complete squadrons ready to deploy on immediate assignment to an aircraft carrier in the event of a national emergency. The Hunters began their distinguished history flying the F-8 Crusader. The F-8 was a supersonic fighter with a variable incidence wing that assisted the pilot during carrier landing. Fighter Squadron 201 commenced 1973 with a bang.... and a boom, and a "swoosh". It was the annual active duty cruise at MCAS Yuma, and the sounds were those of ordnance being expended against a variety of targets. Led by CDR N. M. GILLETTE, the "BOOMERANGS" had been grooming their 12 F8H "Mig Killers" for the big show. January 28th through February 10th found squadron pilots and maintenance men refreshing and requalifying in all aspects of ordnance procedures, from preparation to delivery on target. When the final totals were calculated, the squadron had amassed over 360 flight hours; thousands of rounds of 20mm cannon, zuni rockets and Sidewinder missiles were expended.

Continuing in its desire to provide fleet support, the squadron sent CDR J. T. BEENE and LT's MCDERMID and MANSELL to provide dissimilar ACM for VF-32. For five days, March 12-16, the F8's and F4's from the NAS OCEANA based squadron turned and twisted, zoomed and dived in the traditional dog fight that is the fighter pilots forte. It was excellent training for all aircrews against a dissimilar adversary.

During the months of April and May the squadron concentrated primarily on "in house" training. Emphasis was placed on readiness in an all-weather environment. Pilots intensified their training with the complex air intercept radar. A liaison was established with Bergstrom AFB for use of their GROUND CONTROL INTERCEPT facilities in conjunction with the F8 airborne intercept radar. VF-201 also sent a detachment of F8's to NAS NORFOLK to work with our air group "WILLY FUDDS1' of VAW-207. In another coordinated exercise, opposition against USS INDEPENDENCE. Air group alpha strikes allowed squadron pilots intercept experience with fleet controllers. Reserve Carrier Air Wing Twenty acted as host during the CAG "MINI-GAGGLE", 6 June through 10 June at NAS CECIL, Florida. A detachment of five pilots, LCDR's FLAGG, STAUB, LONEY, WILDMAN, and WOODUL, flew the "Mig Killers" in coordinated air wing Alpha Strikes,-in simulated air combat with air wing A-4's, and in rocket and strafe strikes. March 20 1974 was a first for squadron pilots against the SEPTAR water-borne drone target. All the pilots agreed that firing the Zuni rockets at the speeding boat was a real challenge. The end of June marked the end of Fiscal Year 1973 and the Squadron's first 4000 flight hour year.

July operations were conducted mostly in the Dallas area. Squadron pilots had a chance to "parade-the-colors on a 4th of July flyover at Richardson High School. In an effort to project the Naval Air Reserve image before the public, VF-201 participated in a Memorial Day flyover, the Armed Forces Day Beauty Pagent, where Miss Jean Springer, VF 201 candidate captured 2nd runner-up, and numerous civic club speaking engagements. Active Duty Officers LCDR STOOKEY, officer-in-charge, and LCDR STAUB have been guest speakers for the LIONS Clubs, OPTIMISTS and local church groups throughout the year, additionally the BOOMERANGS participate in a vigorous physical fitness program, including championships in football, tennis, softball, and awards in bowling and volleyball. Other awards for 1973 included the NAVY ACHIEVEMENT MEDAL for AMSC HARDIN and AMS2 BATES, for their outstanding contributions to the squadrons' effectiveness and readiness.

A second weapons deployment was in the mill for squadron personnel; the date was set for the 24th of August and the place, MCAS YUMA, of course. The entire month of August was spent busily meeting deadlines, preparing the sleek fighters for the two week "shoot-out'.

The first round, strangely enough was not at Yuma, but over the sparkling blue waters of the Pacific Missile Range. In an incredibly complex operation involving 17 pilots, 15 targets and tight coordination between the squadron and Pacific Missile Range, all pilots were qualified against AQM targets in two days, without a misfire or lost sortie. Mr. Ray Mason of P.M.R. said that it was one of the smoothest, most well executed exercises he had witnessed. The following week and a half were spent in air-to-air gunnery, air combat maneuvering, air-to-air refueling and air to ground weapons delivery at the Chocolate Mountain Impact Area. The cruise was a tremendous success on the part of all concerned. Of special mention were the efforts of squadron ordnance men, whom earned the Air Wing Commander's Letter of Commendation. No sooner had the squadron returned from active duty than our affiliate, RTU-201, commenced its active duty. This was the second active duty cruise during year 1973 that VF 201 supported. During September squadron maintenance first utilized the new expanded NAS Dallas Naval Air Maintenance Training Detachment facilities.

Additional training was accomplished when a 50 man force was sent to NAS Lemoore, California for firefighting via the new Navy C-9 transport aircraft. It was, without a doubt, the best airlift they had ever experienced. September also found a sad parting between the squadron and its LTV technical advisor, Mr. Ray DeLeva. Ray had been with the squadron since its commissioning in 1970.

An F8 on the catapult and on the NAS Dallas Flight line in 1975.

The last day of September LCDR1s STAUB, and SHARDY, LT1s MCDERMID, MANSELL, and ROSS deployed to Nellis AFB, Nevada to duel with the F4's of the 414th instructor Fighter Weapons School. Five days of intensified tactical air maneuvering against students and instructors yielded more valuable training against a dissimilar adversary. An unusual event was in store for the squadron for October. Airman Apprentice PATSY MARTIN became the first Wave to be assigned a maintenance billet working on the F8 aircraft. She was started in the best possible position to observe the F-8, on the line. From this she hopes to move into the jet mechanic shop, working on the 5-57 power plant.

The date was November 10, 1973 at Hangar 20, NAS Dallas. RADM JOHN GAVAN attended as the guest speaker. The scene was the second change-in-command ceremony for VF-201. Commander Nelson M. GILLETTE had commanded the "Boomerangs" since 3 June, 1972 when he had relieved Commander John LAMERS during the squadron's first change-of-command ceremony. CDR Phillip J. SMITH now relieved CDR GILLETTE as the Commanding Officer and CDR Philip R. PITTS assumed the duties of Executive Officer. It was a gala occasion, with flags flying and dignitaries in attendance, including CAPT HERMAN, NAS Dallas Commanding Officer and CDR ELLIOT, CVWR-20. The "Boomers" initiated another first when a detachment of aircraft and pilots participated in the "College Dart" adversary program at Tyndall AFB, Florida. It was the first time the F-106's from the Air Defense Command had met Naval Reserve Fighters. It was a tremendously successful week of 2 vs 2, 2 vs 4, escorting and patrolling tactics, pitting two nearly equal aircraft in their most demanding roles. It was the highlight of a calendar filled with tactics training, and a fitting way to finish the squadron's operational exercises, Operationally the squadron was confronted with few problems during 1973. Lack of available carrier deck time did not allow pilot refresher in this phase of training. Dissimilar Air Combat Maneuvering against high performance adversaries was ample, however ACM with lower performance/subsonic adversaries were difficult to schedule due primarily to unavailability.

Additionally, insufficient airborne radar intercept training was accomplished due to unavailability of installed operational radars. From a maintenance standpoint the major difficulties centered on supply and parts availability. Also, problems with the J57 P420 fuel control units contributed to aircraft non-availability. Support from the Naval Air Station Intermediate Maintenance Activity on the APQ 149 radar system was less than adequate to insure operational radars for all aircraft. Once again lack of parts was the major contributing factor in down time. In summary, the squadron enjoyed an accident free year that allowed a maximum of training with the assets available. Primarily through its two cruises to MCAS YUMA, pilots, aircraft and maintenance men have combined their capabilities to affect necessary weapons delivery training. Services were provided in support of fleet activities and in providing fleet fighter squadrons with actual dissimilar adversary training. Finally, the squadron experienced its second change of command ceremony when CDR P. J, SMITH relieved CDR N. M. GILLETTE as Commanding Officer. In February 1976 they upgraded to the F-4N Phantom II, beginning an association with the Phantom that was to last 11 years.

F-4 DAYS

VF-201 F-4 PHANTOM

In February 1976 VF-201 upgraded to the F-4N Phantom II, beginning an association with the Phantom that was to last 11 years. However not all of this time was on the F-4N, as in 1984 the squadron transitioned to the F-4S, the most advanced Phantom variant to enter Navy service. In 1984, VF-201 maintained its high state of readiness through numerous deployments. January saw VF-201 making 2 deployments. The first was exercise Constant Peg. Participation in this exercise was designed to expose as many squadron aircrews as possible to realistic adversary training. This objective was met. VF-201 was only the second BESFORON to participate in the exercise. VF-201 then deployed later in January to Tyndall AFB, FL, for an Air Combat Maneuvering Detachment. Major portions of the F-4 Training Matrix were successfully completed during this deployment against various high threat adversaries. All missions were flown on the TACTS range thus allowing in depth debriefs and enhanced training. 3. In February VF-201 commenced its transition from F-4N to the F-4s. Utilizing an innovative and highly viable maintenance training program VF-201 was able to enjoy an extremely successful deployment in May to NAS Miramar for DACT training against F-14, F-5 and TA-4 aircraft. This marked the first squadron deployment with the F4S. Major portions of the F4 training matrix were flown against high threat adversaries on the TACTS with tanker support. The deployment was highly successful in exposing VF-201 aircrews to the increased performance potential of the F4S and the AWG 10A Weapons System. In June VF-201 deployed for CARQUAL and Cyclic Operations on board USS EISEWWER. This deployment demonstrated VF-201's ability to perform the carrier flying mission so crucial to a RESFORON'S mobilization readiness. Despite minimal maintenance support, less than a full complement of aircraft and the ever changing requirements of a CARQUAL evolution, VF-201 qualified 15 of 17 pilots. During the deployment 157 carrier landings were made. COMCVWR-20 ANNUAL ACDUTRA NAS FALLON 18-31 *BUG* 1984. VF-201deployment for COMCVWR-20 Annual ACDUTRA to NBS Fallon marked the completion of VF-201's transition to the F4S. Full mission capability was demonstrated by the deployment of 11 aircraft. Maintenance proficiency was also demonstrated by the broad range of missions successfully carried out. These included the successful firing of 2 AIM 7 E sparrows and 1 AIM 9 H sidewinder missiles with no aborts for radar weapons systems. Additionally the squadron delivered 620 bombs. Twice more VF-201 deployed in 1984. NAS Key West in September where aircrews earned 41 individual E's and 5 qualifications in competitive exercises. This deployment marked the return to the level of ACM proficiency previously enjoyed the F4N with aircrews now demonstrating complete proficiency in the employment of the F4S and the AWG-1OA. December saw VF-201 detaching for the final time to Luke AFB. This deployment was in response to a request from the 405th TTW to provide high performance adversary aircraft for F-15 Eagle replacement aircrew training. This also provided the opportunity for VF-201 aircrews to engage a superior aircraft over land and on a TACTS Range. 7. No squadron can be truly combat ready without an aggressive, visible and comprehensive safety program. VF-201 is justifiably proud of its safety record. The Hunter's philosophy is that an aggressive flight training program need not be incompatible with safe operations, rather that safety and combat readiness go hand in hand. VF-201 ended 1984 with zero class A, B, or C flight mishaps, flight related mishaps, or aircraft ground mishaps. During 1984 the Hunters passed our three year anniversary for accident free flying with over 9000 flight hours flown without mishap. The Hunters commitment to safety was further demonstrated by the following statistics amassed during 1984 achieving a. 107.3% of FY-84 flight hour program flown. Cumulatively deployed 59 aircraft to seven sites for a total of 79 days without incident with a total of 157 carrier landings.

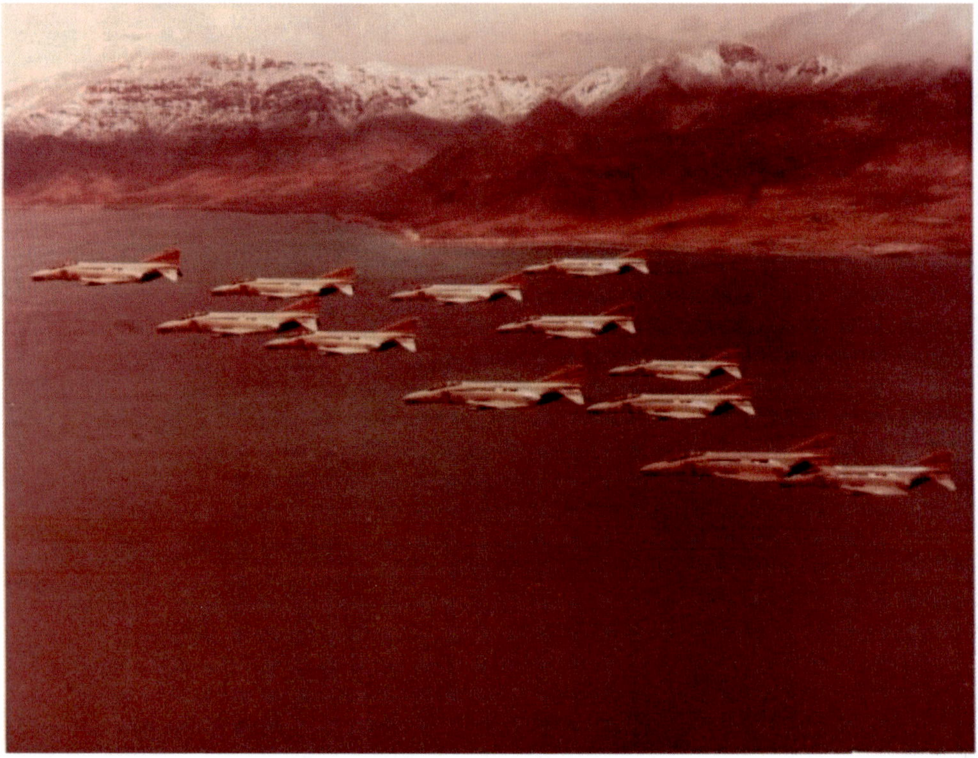

PASSING OF THE TORCH

Let the transition begin. With the Navy moving to a policy of equipping reserve units with equipment as good as that of front line units VF-201 did not have long before the next lot of new equipment arrived. Early in 1987 VF-201 had received their first F-14A Tomcat, Buno. 158634, and continued to receive F-14's until December that year, when the unit's last F-4S, Buno. 155732, was flown to the bone yard at Davis Monthan AFB. Within six months of completing the transition VF-201 carrier qualified onboard the USS Forrestal (CV-59).

F-14 DAYS

In keeping with present policy of giving the reserves equipment of the same quality as their active counterparts, at least some of the machines VF-201 received were fresh off the assembly line. Indeed one of them (Buno.162711) was the last example of the F-14A produced by (Northrop) Grumman, as after this production changed to the F-14A+ (F-14B).

As with fleet squadrons VF-201's role has expanded considerably in the last few years to encompass the new "Strike-Fighter" idea. Thus the squadron is now capable of dropping unguided bombs, cluster munitions, TALD decoys, air laid mines, GBU-10/12/16 series LGB's, practice bombs and marker flares. This capability has been proven in exercises such as the deployment the squadron undertook to NAS Fallon in 1995 as part of training for the whole of the reserve air wing (CVWR-20).

Another new role the squadron has picked up in the last few years is the TARPS mission. This was originally carried out by VF-202 "Superheats", however when the time came for one of CVWR-20's two F-14 squadrons to disestablish the circumstances dictated that VF-201 survived (VF-202's birds were nearer the end of their airframe lives and so would have required either replacement or overhaul).

Another first for VF-201 was its participation in a mine readiness inspection in October 1994, which it passed with flying colors.

Due to cutbacks in active fleet aggressor squadrons VF-201 has picked up the adversary mission as well, providing a range of adversary profiles, from "simple" 1v1 training for less experienced F-14 crews to full fur ball encounters using simulated missiles and kills. This provides realistic training for whole air wings and enables them to conduct realistic composite strike force attacks against a well trained and equipped aggressor force.

The squadron, along with the rest of CVWR-20, is nominally assigned to the USS John F. Kennedy (CV-67) which is now designated as the reserve carrier. Operational circumstances dictated that VF-201 were unable to perform their summer 1996 training detachment upon "their" carrier, instead gaining an opportunity to fly from the Navy's newest operational carrier, the USS John C. Stennis (CVN-74). This was the first time that the whole wing has been assembled together in 7 years. The deployment also featured an opportunity for live weapons firing, with most squadrons using up the majority of their annual live weapon allowance. VF-201 fired 7 AIM-9's, 6 AIM-7's and 1 AIM-54, two more AIM-54's were due to be fired, but due to technical difficulties with the missiles were not used. Showing just how big a part of the F-14's role air-to-ground missions have become, VF-201 also dropped 17,000lbs of ordnance.

The other squadrons that participated in the carrier training were VFA-203 Blue Dolphins, flying the F/A-18A, VFA-204 River Rattlers, also with the F/A-18A, VAQ-209 Star Warriors, flying the EA-6B, VAW-78 Fighting Escargots, with the E-2C, and HS-75 flying the SH-60F. Also aboard was the active Navy unit VS-32 Maulers, flying the S-3B, as CVWR-20 has no S-3 unit assigned to it. VFC-12, flying a single F/A-18B Hornet also participated, this bird carrying the CAG, Captain Charles Askey and allowing him to complete his Carrier Qualification (CQ).

In July 1996 VF-201 deployed to the Naval Air Station at Key West, Florida, to provide dissimilar air training for the active F/A-

18 squadron VFA-106 Gladiators, the East coast Hornet training squadron. This was probably a very popular detachment, for as well as providing plenty of ACM flights, it would have allowed the crews to enjoy the fine Florida weather, whenever they could catch a break that is!

When VF-201 deployed several jets to NAS Oceana in late August/early September 1996 the 2 unused AIM-54's were finally fired, despite the best efforts of two hurricanes to interfere. The visit to NAS Oceana, as well as providing an opportunity to shoot the AIM-54's, enabled VF-201 to participate in the SFARP (Strike Fighter Air Readiness Program) course.

Late 1996 saw VF-201 conducting local operations out of NAS Dallas, preparing for the forthcoming inspection by CVWR-20 command staff.

The flurry of activity in and around Iraq did not lead to VF-201 being activated, but the unit was put on standby, meaning it had to put as many jets as possible in combat configuration. With the F-14 not being the newest of designs getting all 15 ready in such a short space of time was a commendable effort.

In November 1996 VF-201 deployed six F-14's to NAS Fallon, where they provided Dissimilar Air Combat Training (DACT) for CVW-2. This provided excellent training for both VF-201 and CVW-2, especially VF-2, whose F-14D's gave them an edge over VF-201's F-14A's and VFC-13's F-5E/F's.

As the only reserve F-14 squadron remaining (the whole of CVWR-30 being disestablished) VF-201 has a busy schedule, especially as the force draw down means that the reserves now play a more active role and are much more likely to be called upon in times of conflict. VF-201 has risen to this call admirably.

VF-201 has not rested on its laurels for the last few years, continuing its tradition of excellence by winning the 1993 Battle "E" award and the 1994 Chief of Naval Operations (CNO) Safety "S" Award.

With all Pacific F-14 squadrons moving to NAS Oceana it might be assumed that VF-201 would have moved there as well; however this was not the case. Instead during November 1996 the squadron moved to NAS Ft. Worth, a new Joint Reserve Base (JRB) along the lines of the recently reorganized NAS New Orleans. After a celebratory flyby featuring all 14 F-14's VF-201 suspended flying from NAS Dallas on the 25th of November 1996 and began the process of transferring all their aircraft and equipment to the new base. Flying operations restarted from the new base in mid-December.

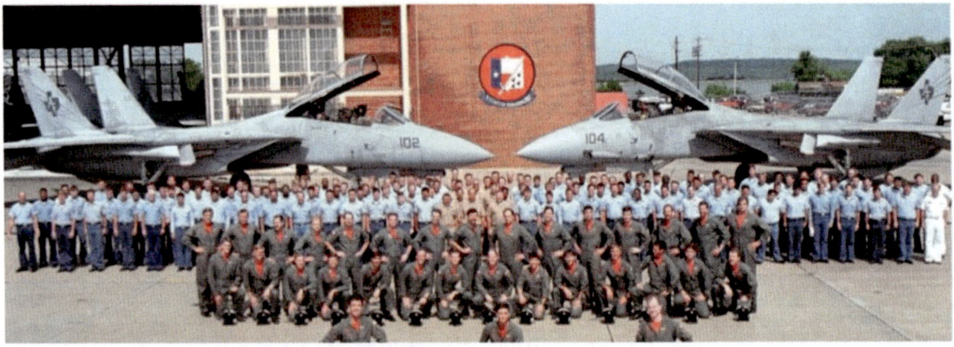
102
104

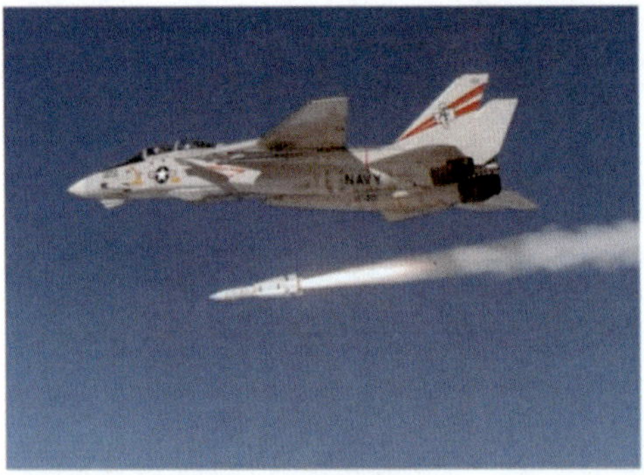
NAVY

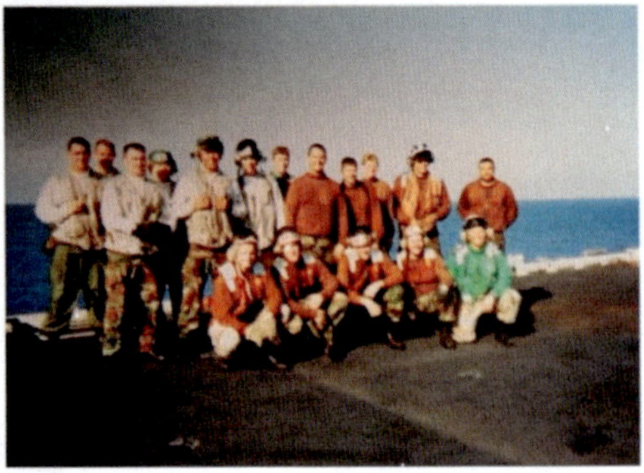

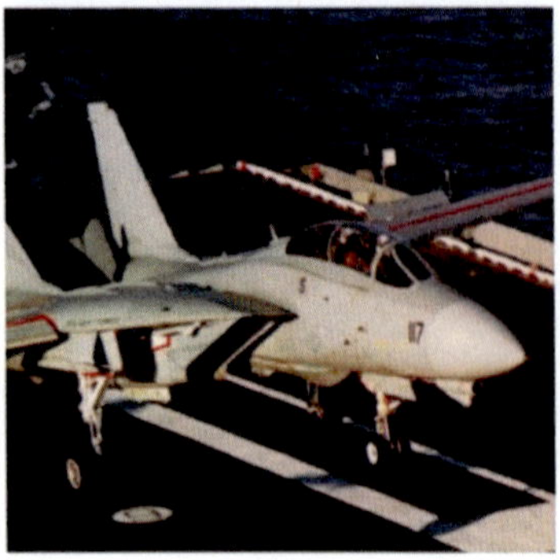

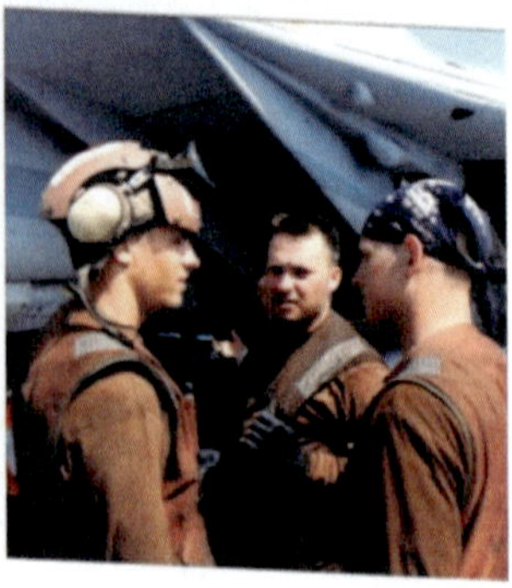

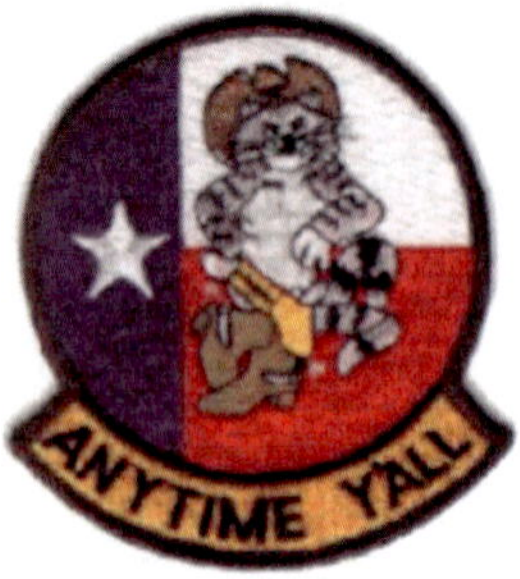
ANYTIME Y'ALL

Martin built the F-16) represent the other three branches of the US armed services, making NAS Ft. Worth a truly Joint base. The squadrons are VR-59 (flying the C-9B), VMGR-234 (flying the KC-130F/T), VMFA-112 (flying the F/A-18A), the 475th FS of the 301st FW (with the F-16C), the 181st AS of the 136th AW, Texan ANG (flying the C-130H) and the 148th Aviation Battalion, Texan Army National Guard (flying the CH-47D).

1997 got off to a busy start for the Hunters, on three days' notice they had to deploy 6 aircraft to Elmendorf AFB, Alaska for Exercise "Arctic Express 1-97". Originally this deployment had been scheduled for an active F-14 squadron, but they were unable to attend and so VF-201 filled the slot. Less than two weeks later, on the 28th of January, VF-201 took part in a scheduled deployment to NAS Fallon, Nevada. This was a live bomb drop exercise and saw the squadron drop 195,000lbs of ordnance and shoot 3500 rounds of 20mm cannon ammo. Also at Fallon during this period was VF-102 "Diamondbacks" flying their brand new updated F-14B's. This version has LANTIRN capability and other upgrades to keep the F-14 current with the expected threats. However some flight tests were still to be completed, so that at this point VF-102 were only able to carry practice bombs on triple ejector racks, rather than "live" ordnance.

Early March has seen the majority of VF-201 deploy to NAS Key West, Florida, for a two week detachment to provide ACM training to new F-14 crews from VF-101. Just a few days earlier, on the 9th of March, aircraft 116 had to make a wire arrested landing at Ft. Worth due to an engine stalling while in an ACM engagement with F-5E's from VFC-13.

Markings for VF-201 are fairly low key, with a silhouette of the Texan state in black, this then having the air wing code 'AF' superimposed on it. Four black lines stretch diagonally from the front base of the tail to the rear top. These may represent the four aircraft that are to be found on the squadron insignia (which also features a sword against the backdrop of a Texan flag). An image of their CAG bird from the mid 80's/early 90's is below, the only change since then has been the deletion of the buff colored nose radome.

VF-201 was equipped with the following aircraft:

BuNo.	Modex	Airframe Hours	Total Landings	Location
158612	100	2529.6	3764	NAS Ft. Worth
158628	101	2775.5	3487	NAS Ft. Worth
158627	102	2027.0	3012	NAS Ft. Worth
158629	103	2503.3	3005	NAS Ft. Worth
158635	104	1778.8	2299	NAS Ft. Worth
158632	105	2055.5	3082	NAS Ft. Worth
158624	106	Unknown	Unknown	Grumman St. Augestine Company
158616	107	Unknown	Unknown	Grumman St. Augestine Company
158634	110	Unknown	Unknown	Grumman St.

				Augestine Company
158633	111	2592.4	3008	NAS Ft. Worth
158618	112	2416.8	2944	NAS Ft. Worth
158620*	114	2539.8	4788	NAS Ft. Worth
161152	115	4813.9	8154	NAS Ft. Worth
159591*	116	3262.5	4155	NAS Ft. Worth
158637*	117	2736.1	4002	NAS Ft. Worth
158614*	120	Unknown	Unknown	Grumman St. Augestine Company

Aircraft marked with a * are the aircraft that are wired to take the TARPS reconnaissance system. All of VF-201's aircraft are Block 140 standard F-14A's, the latest standard.

In 1993, as a result of the downsizing in the armed forces, the Hunters began providing adversary training to fleet strike fighter squadrons. In early 1994, the Hunters expanded their war fighting capability to include the air-to-ground strike missions. Since accepting the challenging air-to-ground mission, VF-201 has delivered over a million pounds of ordnance.

The Hunters also became the first Tomcat squadron to drop mines and participate in a mine readiness inspection. These accomplishments, in combination with the F-14's air-to-air, air-to-ground, Tactical Air Reconnaissance, and adversary missions, provides a good overview of the squadron's versatile [capabilities](). As of the 9th of March 1997, F-14 Buno 161152 had the highest number of hours on the clock, having flown 4813.9 hours. Unfortunately this high total means 115 is past her expected airframe life and so is presently awaiting a "strike" decision to remove her from the Naval inventory. Her high airframe life is unusual because the Buno. indicates that 115 is the newest aircraft the squadron has, however, much of this is due to the fact that a large proportion of this aircraft's life was spent with VF-101, who use their Tomcat's much more than fleet units.

Aircraft at the Grumman St. Augestine Facility are undergoing upgrade, presumably as part of the F-14A/B Block Upgrade, which will give them LANTIRN capability, new cockpit displays, GPS navigation systems and a radar and fire control system upgrade. VF-201 is due to receive four LANTIRN pods during FY97 in replacement for the 4 they were due to receive during FY96. These pods were instead diverted to VF-103, to enable them to work up to full LANTIRN capability in a short space of time. Once the pods and upgraded F-14A's are received VF-201 air and ground crew will begin schooling upon how to load, fly and fight with LGB's, day or night.

WARRANT OFFICER FAST

CWO Fast with an F-14 ready for the USS Kennedy-early 90's. One of the squadrons' most well respected shipmates. He served as a Hunter from August 1973 to December 2000. Longest serving sailor in the squadron.

LCDR JIM BOB SEGAR

LCDR Segars was as a RIO killed in the Dec 1992 mishap Texas during air combat maneuvers with an A-4 Skyhawk. Crashed 30 miles south of Dallas. Former Marine F-4 RIO who transferred over to the Navy because they had a shortage of RIOs with aircraft carrier experience.

THE JIMBO EXPRESS

It was one hell of a flyover that day at NAS JRB Fort Worth.

In January 1999 the Hunters transitioned to the F/A-18 Hornet and were re-designated VFA-201 to signify its multi-mission capability as a Strike Fighter Squadron. The new moniker represents a myriad of changes that have occurred in conjunction with the Hunters transition to the Hornet. The F/A-18 is the Navy's newest front line multi-mission strike fighter aircraft providing the Naval Air Reserve an expanded war fighting capability with improved integration with the Navy's active duty air wings that will serve the Nation well into the new millennium.

F-18 DAYS

In January 1999 the Hunters transitioned to the F/A-18 Hornet and were re-designated VFA-201 to signify its multi-mission capability as a Strike Fighter Squadron. The new moniker represents a myriad of changes that have occurred in conjunction with the Hunters transition to the Hornet. The F/A-18 is the Navy's newest front line multi-mission strike fighter aircraft providing the Naval Air Reserve an expanded war fighting capability with improved integration with the Navy's active duty air wings that will serve the nation well into the new millennium. These were challenging times for us because we had one year to get squadron personnel transitioned and trained to maintain and operate a completely new platform then the F-14. Also the squadron had to re-assign F-14 personnel to other units and bring in a handful of F-18 maintainers and Pilots to convert the squadron over to the new F-18. In the maintenance department we had a F-18 Subject Matter Expert for each rate transfer into the squadron to train the remaining squadron personnel and the new personnel coming into the squadron. As for the pilots some made the transition from the F-14 to the F-18 aircraft and others moved onto to fly different platforms. The F-18s proved to be easier to keep on the daily flight schedule and significantly reduced the maintenance hours to flight hour ratios. For an example the F-14 had a ratio around 65 maintenance hour to one flight hour whereas the F-18 had a 25 maintenance hour to one flight hour ratio. Engine removals on the F-18 would take a crew one hour to remove the engine whereas the F-14 would take 3 to 4 hours for removal. Also the F-18 had bit trouble shooting capabilities and fault code reporting capabilities. But nothing beats an F-14 after burner catapult shot off of an aircraft carrier, absolutely nothing compares to the power and rumbling one can feel up on the flight deck from the F-14.

VFA-201 paint scheme for adversary missions

Hunters having a little fun in Key West Florida on Duvall Street. A great place for liberty.

The only thing guaranteed in life seems to be change and change is exactly what the Hunters conquered. The Hunters new found platform was a crucial element in performing adversary training to all the new pilots flying the F-18. The Hunters found themselves at NAS Key West often meeting up with the Nuggets coming out of NAS Oceana to fly against our pilots who were seasoned Reservists and Top Gun Graduates. The Hunters enjoy much success operating the F-18 aircraft and eventually winning the CVWR-20 Retention Excellence award. Things seemed to be rather routine at the Hunter squadron performing daily sorties in the local MOA, NAS Key West trips training the Nuggets out of NAS Oceana, weekend reserve drills, and a trip or two out to the John F. Kennedy (CV-67) to keep pilots qualified.

911 ATTACKS

On September 11, 2001, 19 militants associated with the Islamic extremist group al-Qaeda hijacked four airliners and carried out suicide attacks against targets in the United States. Two of the planes were flown into the towers of the World Trade Center in New York City, a third plane hit the Pentagon just outside Washington, D.C., and the fourth plane crashed in a field in Pennsylvania. Often referred to as 9/11, the attacks resulted in extensive death and destruction, triggering major U.S. initiatives to combat terrorism and defining the presidency of George W. Bush. Over 3,000 people were killed during the attacks in New York City and Washington, D.C., including more than 400 police officers and firefighters.

I remember September 11, 2001 like it was just yesterday. I was a Maintenance Control Chief back then at the squadron and I decided to take a walk around the squadron spaces visiting the shops to see how the maintenance day priorities were going. During my walk I was approached by another Chief who asked me if I heard what was happening in New York, I replied no I had not heard so the Chief went on to tell me that an aircraft had crashed into one of the towers in New York. After trying to understand exactly what he was saying I decided to walk up to the Duty Office where there was a TV. When I walked into the Duty Office I turned immediately to the TV which was covering the incident. As I watched the TV replay the aircraft flying into the first Tower I was in dismay, I couldn't believe what I was seeing. After a few minutes of watching the TV coverage with the sailor in the Duty Office we both witnessed the second aircraft fly into the other Tower. Both of us were in disbelief on what we just seen on the TV and both immediately acknowledge to one another that we are under attack. Within two minutes the Duty Office phone was ringing. The young sailor picked up the phone and it was our Commanding Officer (CO) calling in. The sailor on duty quickly handed the phone over to me. The CO ordered me to have all the cars removed from the outside of the hangar and establish a watch guard at the gate entrance to the hangar. And he said he was on his way into the squadron. Immediately after getting off the phone with the CO an intercom call was made to remove the cars from outside the hangar. Life as we all knew it would never be the same. Within a few hours it seemed we were working under the direction of North American Aerospace Defense Command (NORAD) and installing live ordnance on our wings fly performing CAP missions over the North Texas area.

RESERVISTS CALLED TO WAR

The word came down. The reservists of VFA-201 were being mobilized for one year. Typically our squadron operated at 40 percent manpower with the TARs (Training and Administration of Reserves) holding down the fort during the month and the reservists coming in for their once a month drill weekends and two weeks of Active Duty Training. Things were pretty much routine, until now. The reservists now had to change their routine, taking leave of absence from their civilian jobs and many other arrangements. Their sacrifices were enormous. With our squadron now 100 percent fully manned the Hunters were now staged to accept the many challenges and call of duty that laid ahead of us in the coming months. I was the Night Shift Maintenance Control Chief and was at getting ready for work when the phone rang at some point in September 2002 around 1300, it was Senior Chief Devanzo from the squadron, when I answered the phone I could tell by the inflection in his voice that something was not good. I immediately asked what was wrong but all he could tell me was that I need to get to the squadron ASAP and that he would tell me when I arrived to the squadron. When I arrived to the squadron I met with Senior Chief Powers. He explained that our squadron has been selected to integrate with CVWR 8, an active duty Air Wing and that the reservists were all being mobilized for one year. He went on to brief me that we were going to deploy with CVWR 8 onboard the USS Theodore Roosevelt (CVN-71). As I took in the news of our squadrons recent orders I reflected back to when I made three cruises on active duty but later transferred to the TAR Navy and never thought I would have to do another cruise, besides I was less than two years from retirement, this can't be happening. He went on to tell me that the squadron was going on 12 hour shifts and that we had one week to transfer all twelve of our F-18s and accept new more moded F-18s. I think I may have said to him sarcastically is that it? So we had an all hands meeting and everything was put out to the troops on what we have been tasked to do. If I recall correctly we shortly went into transferring and accepting twelve F-18s to and from other units in one weeks' time. Something unfrequented in my almost 20 years of service but in true Hunter fashion we got it done. It was a challenging time for the mobilized reservists to. They after all have regular civilian jobs to attend to and now that they have been mobilized for a whole year it was going to be tough for them but they stepped up and met the challenge and integrated with the active duty Hunters flawlessly. For us Tars it was kind've nice to have the reservists with us full time. The reservists in the squadron account for about 60 percent of the total manning for a twelve aircraft F-18 squadron. During normal times the other 40 percent of TARs are operating the squadron. Hats off to the reserves for stepping up and contributing greatly to our new task at hand. We could not have done it without them; after all we are one unit. The next item on the agenda was to go to NAS Fallon Nevada and get qualified with CVWR 8 for two weeks. The pilots had an aggressive training curriculum to complete and we in the maintenance department needed to assure that the available assets were ready for the pilots. I recall it being more then usually cold in Fallon this time around, we worked the maintenance folks pretty hard during that Fallon detachment but once again the Hunters made it happen.

Maintenance Control Fallen Nevada with Senior Chief Powers, Senior Devanzo, Chief Dan Bernhardt and myself during CVWR 8 qualifications in NAS Fallon.

We had to go out to the USS Theodore Roosevelt (CVN-71) next to get are pilots carrier qualified for both day and night which night carrier landings for them was not something they normally had to do since they were in the reserves but now we all are back on active duty. Prior to us going out to sea for CQ we had to get the flight deck personnel trained up on the flight deck operations. The flight Deck and maintenance crew were all season folks but they had not had to go on a full deployment since their active duty days. I was re-assigned as the Night Shift Flight Deck Chief for our squadron prior to going out to sea and was tasked to train and walk through the flight deck (aka the roof) area on top of the roof with all flight deck personnel and conduct familiarization training with the whole crew. Working up on the flight deck is dangerous in itself but working up on the flight deck at night is a totally different animal. Anyways we headed out to sea with the ship and getting used to working under a new CAG. Our pilots got qualified for day and night landings while out to sea and we had our struggles but once again the Hunters made it happen. If I recall right, I had to take myself off of the flight deck due to a severely swollen ankle, heck I could barely make it up the ladder in the cat walk to get to the flight deck but I soon returned back down to my normal duty station, Maintenance Control Chief. I was replaced by Chief Lawrence. While we were out to sea in December 2002 the ships Commanding Officer made an announcement to the ship that we were going to be going back out to sea in January and that we all were to pack our seabags for a 6 month deployment in the case that we don't come back to Norfolk before going on cruise. This was an unusual announcement giving the fact that the cruise prior the ship was out to sea for a straight 159 days, the ship was in need of maintenance and the crew was already worn out. Also, it's customary for a ship to come back to its home port for a few weeks prior to going on a 6 month deployment. Leading up to this point the Hunter Squadron literally worked twelve on and twelve of shifts with only a few days off from September to December.

On October 7th, 2002 history was made

In support of Operation Iraqi Freedom

and in 6 months from activation, delivered over 220,000 lbs of precision guided weapons

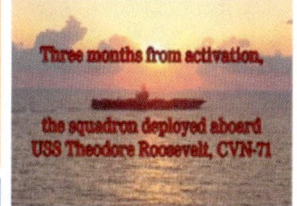

VFA-201 Strike Fighter Squadron 201 was mobilized to active duty

IRAQI FREEDOM

Three months from activation, the squadron deployed aboard USS Theodore Roosevelt, CVN-71

Within 48 hours, all pilots checked on board

In 10 days, maintenance accepted 12 new F/A-18A+ aircraft

One month later, the Hunters completed Air Wing training in Fallon, NV

UNDERWAY

On January 6, 2003 the Hunters got onboard the USS Theodore Roosevelt (CVN-71) in Norfolk Virginia to join the ship's crew and CVWR 8 for cruise they went underway. For many this was going to be their first cruise but for the reservists and some of us TARS we have been here before. In the mean time I was sent a few days earlier to NAS Oceana prior to the ship leaving Norfolk with an advance Detachment which included 4 maintainers and a maintenance cell phone to get ready for the jets to arrive in NAS Oceana for staging while the pilots awaited for the overhead message to come in to fly onboard the ship. When my crew and I showed up to NAS Oceana I met up with maintenance Chief from one of the squadrons at the base and he gave us a little area in his Maintenance Control where we could operate out of when the jets arrived. As the jets starting to arrive on NAS Oceanas crew would pump up the struts and tires for carrier pressure settings, fuel the jets, give them a fresh Daily and Turnaround Inspection and fix any squawks that the pilots wrote up. As the NAS Oceana flight line started filling up with Hunter jets one of the other Maintenance Chiefs came over and asked me where the rest of my maintenance crew, (I had with me Petty Officers Ferraro, Bartz, Hainlin I believe and one other maintenance person which I can't recall his name right now) I replied I hope they're on the flight line taking care of the jets cause I want to go get some beer and eventually get to relax for the night. He said well you only have 4 maintainers and I said yes I have four. He replied with disbelief "4 maintainers for 11 jets"? I laughed and said we "Got this" but if I need any help would you be willing to assist? The Chief said whatever I wanted just ask. (we only had 11 jets at that point because aircraft 204 was stuck back in Fort Worth due to a tail scag fuel leak....You're not supposed to fly a jet onboard the carrier if its' leaking fuel. If you do as soon as that jet hits the flight deck it will go down to the hangar. The Air Boss doesn't like fuel leaks up on his flight deck. A few days had passed before the pilots finally got the overhead message to fly onboard so the jets launched out of Oceana and my crew and I went onto Puerto Rico. In the meantime the ship and crew were getting ever drill possible thrown at them and being evaluated by the Fleet Readiness Inspectors before we could steam across the pond (Atlantic). My crew and I showed up to Puerto Rico, checked into the barracks and later that day went to VC-8s hanger to check in and get a space for us. During this time the CVWR 8 Maintenance Officer (MO) somehow got the squadrons' maintenance cell number to the phone I had and was calling me from the ship tasking me with getting my guys to troubleshoot other CVWR (CAG) 8 jets because we were the only maintenance folk's period in Puerto Rico at the time. Everyone else was onboard the ship off the coast of Florida or Puerto Rico somewhere. My guys would give their best guess at maintenance issues on CVWR 8s F-14s, S-3s etc…I would then call the CAG MO and tell him what the possible issues were, he then would fly out other squadrons maintenance folks from the ship to fix there jets. Anyways I had been on the phone with various people from the ship from our squadron as well. Mostly was speaking to our Maintenance Master Chief Joe Blackburn majority of the time handling things he wanted us to do while we were in Puerto Rico awaiting on our aircraft 204 to come in from Fort Worth. The crew back in Fort Worth got aircraft 204 repaired and soon after Commander Dewalt showed up with aircraft 204 in Puerto Rico. When he showed up he said he had a planning Link Failure Caution. He also said that he had an overhead time in just a few hours. He wrote the squawk up and went to go get some food. Well the guys started troubleshooting the Planning Link Failure and Petty Officer Bartz came to me and said we would need to swing the gear after his repair for him to sign it off. Well that created a problem because we had no room in VC-8s hangar and on and on. We all talked about it (the 5 of us) and decided to take the jet out to VC-8s flight line. Petty Officer Ferraro and the guys jacked the plane up and one of the guys jumped in the cockpit and started the APU. With the APU running and aircraft 204 on VC-8s flight line we swung the gear. One part I guess I have left out is VC-8 was conducting flight operations on the flight line, some of the looks we got from VC-8s pilots as they taxied by us looking at our F-18 up on jacks on their flight line were priceless. Commander Dewalt showed up a few hours later and asked how we fixed the caution. I explained we did a full operational check of the gear and some improvising to get the gear swing done. We both grinned and he took the jet to the ship. Shortly thereafter it was time for us to fly onboard the ship but before we did the CAG MO called and said I was now the new CAG 8 Maintenance Chief for shore and I was to fly to Spain next. Well my guys got on the C2 and flew off to the ship. After my crew left I called Master Chief Blackburn and told him what the CAG MO had told me, after a minute or two after he calmed down he said he will deal with the CAG MO and that I was to get on the next C-2 and get to the ship because he needed me in Maintenance Control. Before I got on the C-2 to get back to the ship I went to the store on base that day and picked up the requested items from guys who wanted various things from the ship and got on the next C2 the following day. After landing on the ship I walked off the Flight Deck and started down the 03 level up forward where our Maintenance Control was and no kidding the first person I see on the 03 level is the CAG MO. He stops, looks at me and ask what the heck am I doing onboard the ship, he said you're supposed to be heading to Spain. As things went the CAGMO and I walked up forward together to our Maintenance Control and the CAGMO and Master Chief

OIF OPERATIONS

Blackburn had words let's just say. The ship left the Port of Norfolk and steamed south towards the coast of Florida performing required drills as a ships company and Fleet to get Combat Readiness qualified.

The Hunters of VFA-201 was the seventh tactical Navy reserve squadron mobilized since the Korean War (three East Coast based and three West Coast based USNR squadrons were activated during the Vietnam war on 28 January 1968), ***but we were the only squadron to actually deploy for combat operations in Naval Air Reserve History.*** After completing the Strike Fighter Advanced Readiness Program (SFARP) from their home base in Fort Worth and Carrier Air Wing Eight coordinated strike detachment in Fallon, Nevada, they deployed on board the USS Theodore Roosevelt (CVN-71) from 6 January to 29 May 2003, where they received numerous awards for their performance over Iraq during the first phases Of Operations Iraqi Freedom. In fact, the squadron delivered over 220,000 pounds of ordnance on Iraq targets. Additionally, VFA-201 had an unprecedented 84.6 target acquisition rate during Iraqi Freedom and won the Carrier Air Wing Eight landing grade competition for their entire workup and combat deployment. Eighteen of the nineteen pilots deployed were graduates of TOPGUN.

On March 22, 2003 the Hunters launch into History as part of CVWR 8 performing the first Air Strike "SHOCK AND AWE" from the USS Theodore Roosevelt (CVN-71) off the coast of Syria in the Mediterranean Sea in support of Operation Iraqi Freedom (OIF). The missions were essentially 7 hour flights. Once the aircraft took off from the catapult it would tank twice in the clouds from a KC-135 over Turkey to get over to Northern Iraq and upon return tank twice again and land on the ship with pitching deck of over 20 feet in a rough sea state and often taking lightning strikes while on approach which sometimes knocked out the aircraft navigational systems. Hats off to our Pilots for their Bravery.

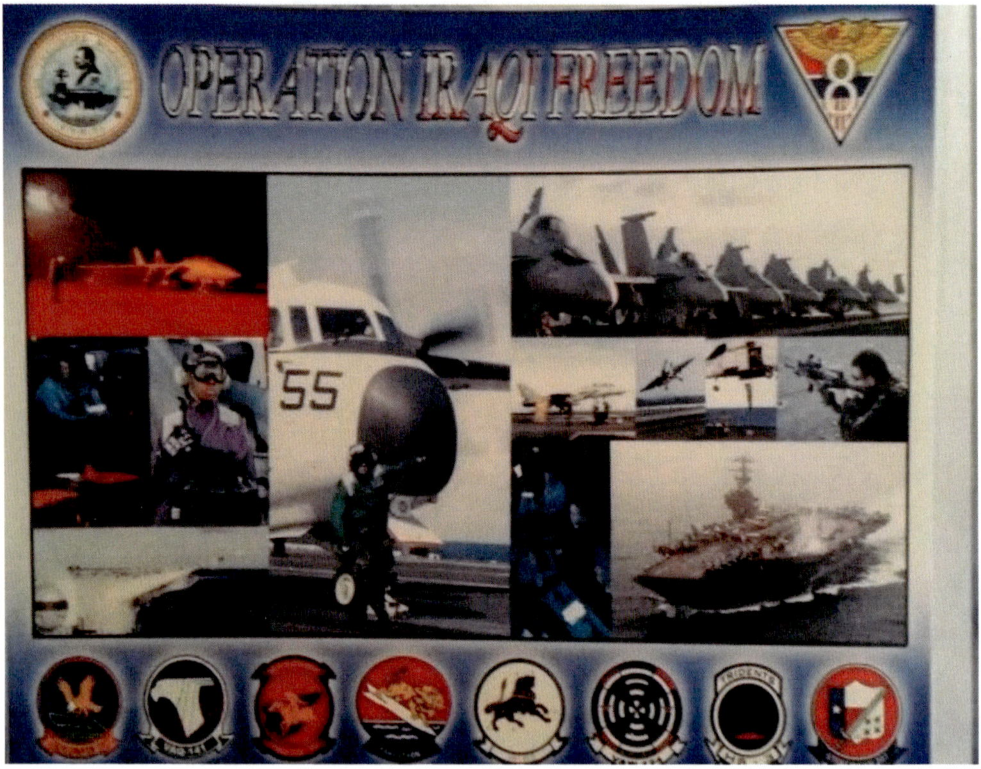
OPERATION IRAQI FREEDOM
8
55

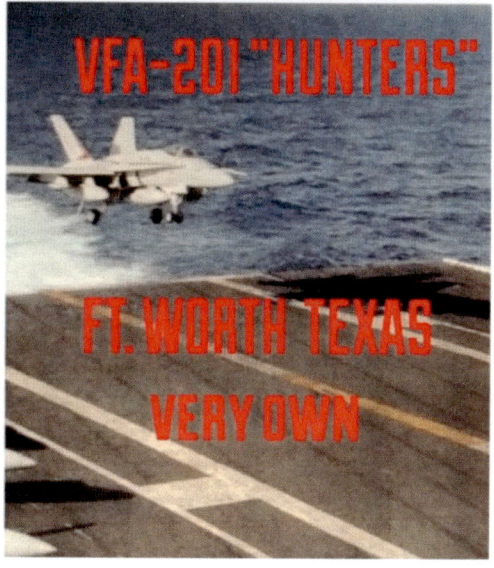

Hunters up on deck of USS Theodore Roosevelt (CVN-71) during Shock and Awe missions.

Hunter Crew

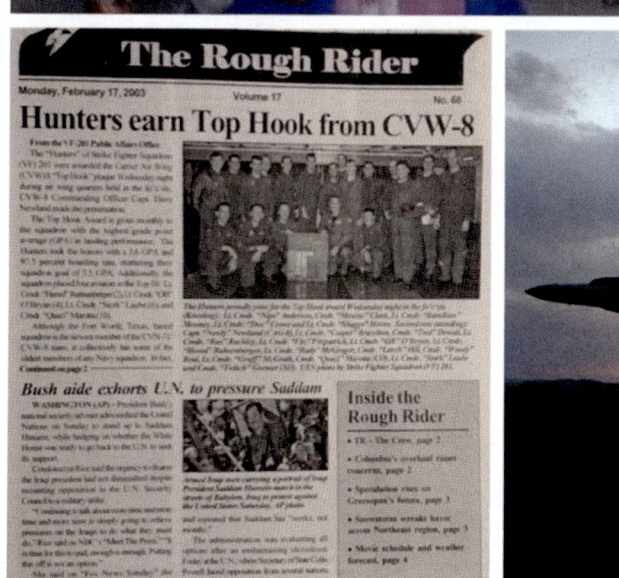

THE HUNTER PILOTS. THE BEST OF THE BEST.

Hunter Chiefs. "If it was easy everyone else would already be doing it."

These were typical markings on all our jets during the Shock and Awe Missions the Hunters performed. The air strikes off the coast of Syria into Northern Iraq only lasted two weeks. The pilots ran out of ground targets partially due to the accuracy of our weapons, Laser Guided and GPS Guided missiles. Our air strikes provided needed support in order to allow the ground special forces and troops to move further North in Iraq. The Hunters proved to the rest of the Navy that a reserve squadron if called upon can fill in as needed and join up with the active duty Air Wings.

The Rough Rider

Tuesday, December 17, 2002 — Volume 17 — No. 26

First Classes show holiday spirit

By JO1(SW) Rob Kerns

In a very special dinner meal Monday, many of USS Theodore Roosevelt's (CVN 71) first class petty officers revisited their roots by washing plates in the scullery, taking out trash from the mess decks and wiping down tables.

By rolling up their sleeves and helping out, the first classes raised $1,004 to help out TR Sailors who can't afford to buy gifts for their loved ones during the holiday season.

Crewmembers were given the opportunity to nominate first classes for mess duty by buying votes for a dollar. TR sailors nominated first classes with donations ranging from $1 to $190.

The top 10 first classes were sent to the scullery, the next 10 were assigned trash duty and the remaining 48 nominated first classes had to wipe up tables.

"I couldn't have been happier with the turnout," said First Class Petty Officer Association President, Disbursing Clerk 1st Class Wendell Stephens. "We have done this before, but never with these kind of numbers."

Leading in the donations was Operations Specialist 1st Class Robert F. Regan with $208.

Navy Counselor 1st Class Grant Stickney, left, and Personnelman 1st Class Sean Hughes, wipe down tables on the aft mess decks of USS Theodore Roosevelt (CVN 71) to support their shipmates. USN photo by PH3 Phillip Nickerson.

"I was surprised I had that much money put on me," said Regan. "This is for a really good cause, so I'm more than willing to wash some plates and silverware to help out."

Donations for the FCPOA Gift Basket came from all over the ship. TR's Executive Officer Capt. Terry Kraft was even seen making a donation.

"TR Sailors helping TR Sailors is a great example of what the holiday season is about," said Kraft. "It also gives me the opportunity to see my first classes working," he added with a smile.

Some of the nominated first classes had no idea they were nominated but were happy to have the opportunity to help out their shipmates.

"I was stoked to see my name on the list," said Navy Counselor 1st Class Grant Stickney. "We have to remember that the holidays are about giving to others, and this is just another way to do that."

VFA-201 "Hunters" make history on board TR

By JO2 Kirk Boxleitner

A group of Naval reservists from Texas are making history on the decks of USS Theodore Roosevelt (CVN 71).

For the first time since the Korean War, an entire Naval Air Reserve Squadron has been deployed on board an aircraft carrier.

Strike Fighter Squadron 201 (VFA-201), based at Naval Air Station Fort Worth Joint Reserve Base in Texas, was ordered to active duty by President George W. Bush, as a unit of Carrier Air Wing Eight (CVW-8) embarked on board TR.

"The first week of October, I got the call at work," said Strike Fighter Tactics Coordinator Lt. Cmdr. Rob "Rudy" McGregor, a selective reservist from Twin Bridges, Mont., who works as an engineering consultant for Lockheed-Martin. "It wasn't a total surprise, though since the possibility had been talked about for a couple of months."

"Originally, we'd heard that Carrier Air Wing Nine had an opening for an FA-18 squadron, but VFA-22 filled that," said Maintenance Master Chief Joe Blackburn, of Castro Valley, Calif., who has served the past six of his 24 years in the Navy as a selective reservist. "Then Carrier Air Wing Eight created the hole that we're filling now."

"When our commanding officer let us know, in the squadron's hangar bay, I was excited, and a little nervous, and I still am," said Aviation Ordnanceman Airman Jamie Shield, of Winona, Minn., who will commemorate her two-year anniversary as

Continued on page 2

Inside the Rough Rider

- TR - THE CREW, page 2
- NYC transit strike off as talks continue, page 4
- Stallone ready for "Rocky" redux, page 6
- Movies and weather, page 8

THE LEGENDARY HUNTERS OF TEXAS

ABOARD USS THEODORE ROOSEVELT, At Sea (NNS) -- Strike Fighter Squadron (VFA) 201, currently deployed aboard USS Theodore Roosevelt (CVN 71), is the 2002 winner of the Commander, Air Wing 20 Noel Davis Award, the Reserve aviation Battle "E."

The award recognizes the top squadron in several categories, including number of flight hours, number of arrested carrier landings, safety, readiness and training, ordnance delivered, pilot qualifications, full-mission-capable aircraft, enlistment advancement and retention, and hazard reports (HAZREPS).

"Ever since we transitioned to F/A-18s in 1999, we've been striving to always do better," said Cmdr. Tom Marotta, VFA-201 commanding officer. "We always say 'Hunter Pride, Hunter Spirit and Hunter Excellence.' I think we've proven we strive for excellence."

VFA-201, based out of Naval Air Station, Joint Reserve Base, Fort Worth, Texas, is the first Reserve squadron to be called to active duty since the Korean War, and the seniority of its staff may well have played into the selection in the Battle "E." According to Marotta, squadron pilots experience averages 2,700 flight hours, and some enlisted personnel have been with the Hunters as long as 17 years.

"We have lots of experience as a team," Marotta said. "All we needed was some boat experience."

And that experience is what Roosevelt and Carrier Air Wing (CVW) 8 provided to the Hunters.

Since activating in mid-October, the Hunters have accumulated more than 2,600 flight hours, more than 1,600 sorties and more than 1,000 arrested landings aboard Roosevelt.

"Their performance merits their selection," said Capt. David Newland, commander, Carrier Air Wing (CVW) 8. "They transitioned to 12 new planes, then got the call and fully activated the squadron two weeks before joining the wing. This award just goes to show how hard 201 is working."

Marotta praised the team spirit within the squadron and within the Roosevelt/CVW-8 team. He noted that the Hunters were hand picked to activate because of the desire to deploy as a team, not a group pieced together from several squadron's volunteers.

"VFA-87 and VFA-15 have worked with us from the start," he said. "This has not been a 'sink or swim' group. It's a 'hey, we need to help each other' group. If we need something, another squadron helps us, and we do the same in return. Everyone's working together."

HOMECOMING

On May 29, 2003 the USS Theodore Roosevelt (CVN-71) returned home after leaving on work ups in January 6, 2003 the ship was scheduled to return back to its Home Port of Norfolk before going on cruise but circumstances forced the ship to steam across the Atlantic instead answering the to the Call of Duty to perform Shock and Awe Airstrike Missions in support of OIF. The ship was now returning from two War deployments in 12 months.

A Hero's welcome home back at NAS JRB Fort Worth Texas on May 29, 2003.

It hasn't been done in 50 years. Not since the Korean War has an entire Naval Reserve strike fighter squadron been activated and deployed at sea.

Yet history has a tendency to repeat itself.

The "Hunters" of Strike Fighter Squadron (VFA) 201 returned to Texas May 29, after an impressive six-month performance in support of Operation Iraqi Freedom. From the decks of USS Theodore Roosevelt (CVN 71), the Hunters flew more than 1,000 sorties, seamlessly joining active-duty counterparts in the war on terrorism.

Hundreds of family members, relatives, federal and local dignitaries, and other base personnel greeted the "Hunters" with waving flags, cheers and tears, as the two C-40A aircraft carrying most of the squadron members taxied closer and closer to the waiting throng. Minutes later, the squadron's returning pilots flew directly overhead in their F/A-18 Hornets, and again, the waving flags and cheers erupted. It was a news media field day, as families and friends rushed forward, as the returning Sailors and pilots left their planes.

"The Navy was in dire need of a fighter squadron to do this assignment, and 201 was the team to do it," says Capt. Stanley O'Connor Jr., commander of Carrier Air Wing Reserve 20.

O'Connor says the Hunters validated the role a Reserve strike squadron can perform, saying, "There's so much to tell about the great things they accomplished."

Lt. Cmdr. David "Sluggo" Moore, a pilot for VFA-201, says that any success in the air was due to the work on deck. "Personally, I'm most proud of the maintenance effort our Reservists put forth," he said.

Preparing the Hunters' F/A-18A Hornets by adding mission-specific equipment and keeping the planes in top shape came naturally to VFA-201 crew members, who've already earned three "Golden Wrench Awards" for best air wing maintenance.

Taking their Reserve show on the road was apparently no problem for the Hunters, as the pilots earned Top Hook honors for the cruise, winning all three "line periods" - grading periods that rate the squadrons' landings. The squadron as a whole earned a fourth Battle "E" Efficiency Award for combat readiness.

Still, no success at sea compares to the joy of coming home.

"It's great to be home. Home's where my heart is," sighs Aviation Maintenance Administration man 2nd Class Vickie Meriwether, minutes after landing at Naval Air Station Joint Reserve Base Fort Worth.

"It's good to be home!" echoes Aviation Machinist's Mate 1st Class Travis Redenbaugh, adding, "I'd really like to say thanks for all the support from back home - all the letters, the e-mails. It really helped."

Reservists in Strike Fighter Squadron 201 Return to Families After Five Months at Sea

From the Star-Telegram
NAS News Photos by Tony Bliss

They lurked off the Virginia coast all morning, then they waited the afternoon out for thunderstorms to clear. But at 6:40 p.m., the wait was finally over.

The landing steps dropped from the two C-40 airplanes, and Strike Fighter Squadron 201's historic five-month cruise ended in a mob of roses, tears and long embraces.

"The last two days were the longest we had," said Jason Manning, a petty officer second class, who was greeted by his wife and two children at the squadron's hangar at Naval Air Station Fort Worth.

Called to active duty in October and sent to sea aboard the USS Theodore Roosevelt in early January, the squadron participated in dozens of bombing missions during the war in Iraq and perhaps forever raised the profile of naval reservists. But that seemed a long way off Thursday evening.

"I'm going to just enjoy being with my family," said Jorge Valenzuela, who left his home in Keller and job in manufacturing to work on the flight deck. "I want to sleep in my own bed, and I want to be able to take a shower without shower shoes."

Doug Williams, a petty officer first class who took leave as an engineer at Lockheed Martin, planned to relish the sound of every "Daddy" spoken by his daughters.

After the 200 enlisted sailors landed, the squadron's pilots flew in a 12-plane formation low over the hangar, landing as their families ran to meet them.

"It was a nice short cruise by Navy standards," said Cmdr. Doug Beale, a pilot who typically flies for American Airlines. "But when you're away from your family, it always seems like an eternity."

Originally called up to fill a gap in Carrier Air Wing 8, the squadron and the Theodore Roosevelt left home five months earlier than scheduled because of the war in Iraq.

It was the first time since the Korean War that a tactical Naval Reserve squadron was mobilized and sent to sea on a carrier.

Capt. Stan O'Connor, who commands tactical reserve squadrons nationwide, said Squadron 201 distinguished itself by besting every squadron on the ship in landings, by taking a lead role in missions, by helping plan attacks and by its initiative in maintenance.

"The Navy has been resistant to using the reserves this way," said O'Connor, an active-duty officer. "This time, they had to. And 201 hit the proverbial home run."

Operating out of the eastern Mediterranean Sea, the squadron's pilots entered the war on March 22, flying through the Sinai Peninsula into Iraq.

For the remainder of their 270 sorties the next three weeks, they flew into northern Iraq through Turkey, supporting special operations troops and the 173rd Airborne Brigade.

Cmdr. Tom Marotta, the squadron commander and a pilot for Federal Express, praised the squadron's maintenance and ordnance personnel, saying their performance was unbelievable. The squadron made 100 percent of its combat sorties, meaning none had to be scrapped for maintenance problems.

"Every airplane we needed airborne made it to the theater, and every bomb exploded on target," he said.

The squadron had to overcome numerous obstacles to go to sea in the first place. Its planes had to be replaced because they were no longer seaworthy. The pilots and mechanics had to learn new and more complex weapons systems. And they had to ramp up their training to catch up with the active-duty units.

The squadron also did it with a considerable number of enlisted sailors who had never been on active duty and never been on a long cruise.

By the war's end, the squadron's pilots flew more than 1,100 hours of combat and dropped more than 200 precision-guided bombs and 220,000 pounds of ordnance. ✪

HIGH ACHIEVEMENT

THE CREDIT BELONGS TO THE MAN WHO IS ACTUALLY IN THE ARENA, WHOSE FACE IS MARRED BY DUST AND SWEAT AND BLOOD, A MAN WHO KNOWS THE GREAT ENTHUSIASMS AND GREAT DEVOTIONS, WHO SPENDS HIMSELF IN A WORTHY CAUSE; WHO IN THE END KNOWS THE TRIUMPH OF HIGH ACHIEVEMENT, AND IF HE FAILS, AT LEAST FAILS WHILE DARING GREATLY SO THAT HIS PLACE SHALL NEVER BE WITH THOSE COLD TIMID SOULS WHO KNOW NEITHER VICTORY NOR DEFEAT

Teddy Roosevelt

HUNTERS

INTO THE SUNSET – DECOMMISIONING

The Hunters' long season in North Texas is over. The Hunters of Strike Fighter Squadron 201 have prowled the skies over North Texas, leaving contrails from the supersonic engines of Crusaders, Phantoms, Tomcats and, finally Hornets. March 24, 2007 marked the last flight for the F/A-18s. CDR Beal, the squadron's last Commanding Officer wanted the celebration to be a celebration. I was in attendance that day and for me it was a sad day. I asked why they would close down our squadron and not a different reserve squadron. After all we were mobilized and proven in combat operations already. Perhaps it was politics not sure that decision was way above my pay grade as a Chief. That day the Commanding Officer of Naval Station Dallas, Captain Ian McIntyre, credits the Hunters with "Putting reserve aviation on the map" with their performance over in Iraq in 2003. Past Commanders, who flew out of Naval Air Station Dallas, recall the days when the pilots and crew chiefs had experience in Korea and Vietnam. "For 50 plus-years, there has been a presence of Navy Fighters in the Dallas-Fort Worth area," said retired Captain Ed Flynn, who commanded the squadron from 1982 to 1984. "That's going away now. It's sad." Navy Reserve aviation Units have been on the chopping block in recent years as the Navy struggles with budget pressures and expensive hardware needs. In the Hunters' case, the active-duty force needs the airplanes. New F/A-18 models are not being purchased fast enough to replace worn out by demanding operations.

Any thought that the Hunters, who owned one of the most distinguished combat records of the any Navy Squadron, might be shielded from budget cuts slipped away when the Navy selected the squadron for shutdown. Only two reserve combat hornet squadrons remained open nationwide. U.S. Rep. Kay Granger, R-Fort Worth, and Senators Kay Bailey Hutchison and John Cornyn of Texas protested the move but could do little to alter the Defense Departments plans. Most of the squadron's planes have already been sent to units in Virginia, California and Nevada, for Commander Beal, who served in the squadron for eight years its akin to "cutting off a limb." The Fort Worth Naval Air Station was left with five flying squadrons. Only one of them will be Navy Reserve, and it's a cargo squadron. Paul Payne, a former Commanding Officer of the Hunters believed that sacrificing the reserve squadrons to solve budget problems is shortsighted. Paul Payne further stated the squadron "needs to be remembered as a squadron that met their nation's call and did it extremely well. The Hunters were praised as the best fighter squadron in the Air Wing when they deployed for the OIF Shock and Awe Air Strike Missions into Northern Iraq.

69

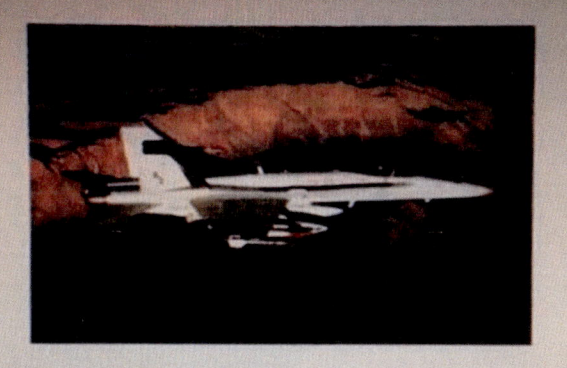

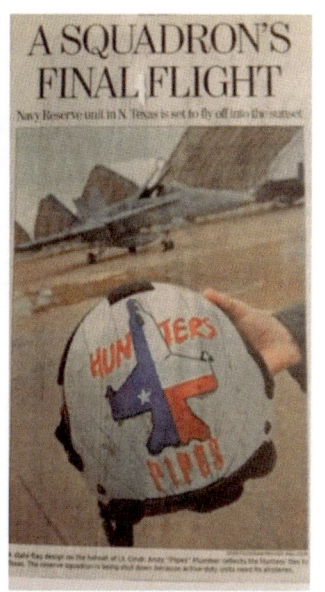

HUNTERS ROSTER OIF / SHOCK AND AWE MISSIONS

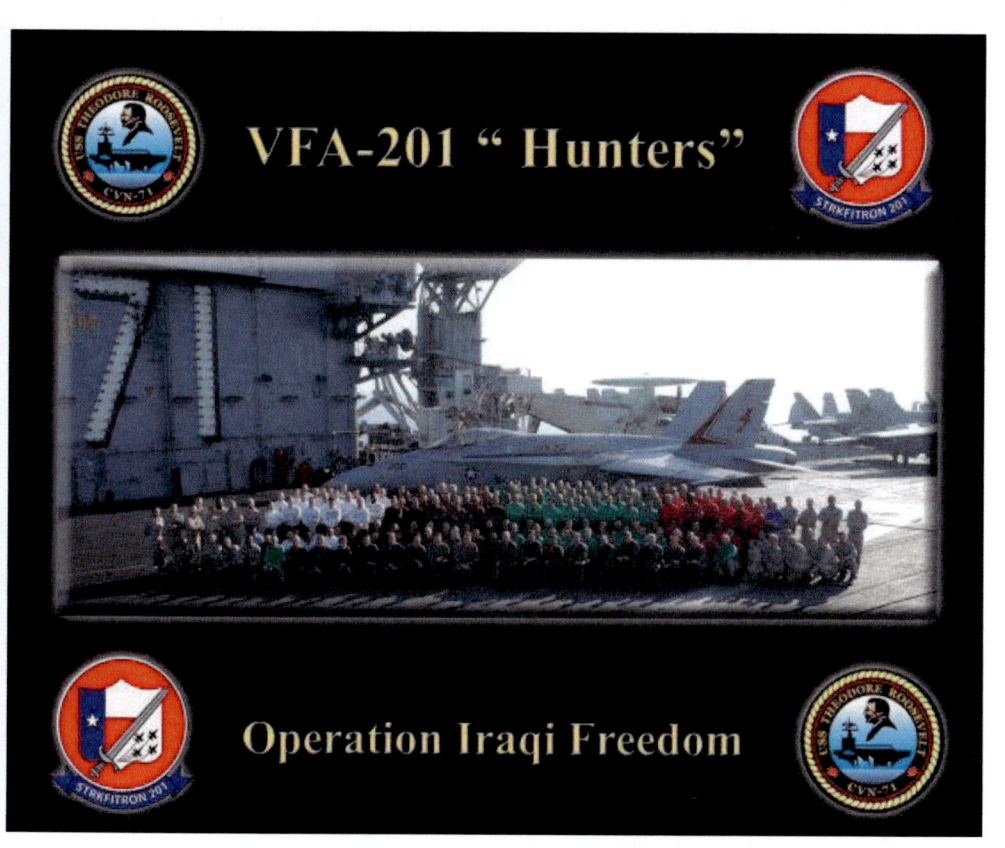

CDR THOMAS W. MAROTTA (CO), CDR SHAWN R. GRENIER (XO), CMC RICHARD L. JOHNSON CDR DOUG BEAL, CDR SEAN CLARK, CDR ROD DEWALT, CDR EDWARD H. HILL, LCDR NICHOLAS M. ANDERSON, LCDR RAY W. ARNOLD, LCDR MARK D. BRAZELTON, LCDR TALMADGE L. CROWE, LCDR PAUL A. LAUBE, LCDR JOHN J. MCGRATH, LCDR ROB R. MCGREGOR, LCDR JOHN P. MOONEY, LCDR STEPHEN F. O'BRYAN, LCDR SEAN A. RACKLEY, LCDR MARTIN R. RUMRILL, LCDR MICAHEL RUSHENBERGER, LT RUSSEL S. JONES, CWO3 KEN H. LAYRE, AVCM JOE BLACKBURN, AMCS DAVID G. DEVANZO, ATCS (AW) LESLIE J. GERRARD, ATCS PATRICIA M. HELMICH, AMCS DAVID L. KILL, ADCS (AW) RAYMOND M. POWERS, YNC (AW) ARON A. BATISTE, AMC (AW) DANIEL P. BERNHARDT, HMC KENNAM R. BOURG, AMEC (AW) GARY D. CHAPIN, ATC (AW) MELISSA

CHILDERS, ADC (AW) PAUL R. FREEMAN, AEC (AW) JOE L. HIGGINS, PNC MARLENE D. HUMPHREY, ASC, BRADLEY D. JONES, ATC DAVID S. LAWRENCE, AMC DAVID A. MASON, YNC (AW) DWAYNE A. MITCHELL, AEC EDWARD E. MULLENIX, ATC MICHAEL F. MURNANE, AMC (AW) WESLEY D. OSBURN, AZC JOESPH K. PARASCANDOLO, AOC (AW) SCOTT M. SMITH, AEC (AW) PERRY WARD, SR1 STEVE, PRI JAMES P. BLACK, III, AMI (AW) MICHAEL S. BROWN, AM1 (AW) GERALD A. CAMPBELL, AME1 MARK A. CUPPS, AM1 SCOTT E. DANIELS, AE1 (AW) LAURIE A. DAVIS, AE1 EDWARD DOBBS, AM1 ROBERT J. FERRERO, AT1 WILLIAMS A. FERGUSON, AK1 (AW) RACHEL E. GUZMAN, AE1 WILLIAMS S. HARRELL, AE1 RUSSELL E. HAWKINS, AM1 (AW) MICHAEL J. HVASS, AME1 DARRIN D. LEE, AD1 DANIEL E. MARTELLE, AZ1 TOMMY MATA, III, AT1 VICTOR MOLINA, AT1 (AW) RICKY L. MORGAN, YN1 (AW) ROBERT A. MOSHER IS1 DAVID R. PARRISH, AT1 RICHARD M. RADIGAN, ADI BOBBY J. REED, AD1 TRAVIS Y. REDENBAUGH, AME1 DONNELL R. THARP, JR, AK1 DARRELL W. UTECH, AD1 JAMES H. VANDERBECK, AT1 (AW) WULF H. WERNER, AE1 (AW) DOUG W. WILLIAMS, AT1 TRAVIS ZAMORA, AT2 GREG W. ALLEN, AE2 ENRIQUE ALVARADO, AM2 ROGER C. ANZUALDA, AM2 LIOYD F. BARTON, AE2 JERONIMO J. BARTZ, AM2 PHILLIP L. BATES, AM2 JEFFREY P. BOBO, AM2 JEFFREY L. BROWN, AM2 DARYL K. BRUNSON, AO2 STEPHEN BUCKHORN, AM2 DAVID T. CHAMBERLAIN, AE2 (AW) BRIAN F. GALLAGHER, PR2 KEVIN W. GFELLER, AM2 MICHAEL A. GOBEA, SK2 SEAN P. HALE, AD2 JEFFREY R. HAMS, AO2 JOHN D. HURT, AE2 VICTOR M. CANO, SK2 BENITO H. CARABAJAL, AME2 EDGAR E. CASTENEDA, AT2 DONALD L. CRAIG, IS2 MICHAEL G. DEIRIE, AE2 CESAR O. JOHNSON, AO2 LANCE A. KEELING, PR2 BRIAN H. LEVERETT, AD2 ROBERTS W. LYONS, MS2 ERROL L. MALCOLM, AE2 JASON M. MANNING, IT2 RUDY MARTINEZ, AD2 CHRISTOPHER J. McREE. AZ2 VICKIE E. MERRIWEATHER, AT2 MICHAEL L. MILLS, AT2 PATRICK M. MINOGUE, AM2 CHARLES W. MURPHEY, AME2 KERRI NOACK, AM2 BRIAN E. ORTH, AT2 STEPHEN M. PARSONS, AM2 ANTHONY L. PATTERSON, PN2 MICHAEL D. PORTER, MS2 LEONARD PROESTLY, AD2 LEONARD L. PRUITT, AM2 (AW) DANIEL J. QUEEN, AS2 JOHN G. ROSE, SK2 MARK G. SANTOYO, AD2 DONALD M. SIMMONS, AT2 JOHN A. SMITH, AE2 LYLE A. SMITH, AME2 ERIC L. SOYEZ, AE2 TONY L. STONE, AD2 MARK E.

TANNER, AT2 RICHARD E. TORREY, AS2 WILLIAM C. TWOMBLY, JR, AM2 SHAWN A. VANDERHOUWEN, AO2 ROBERT G. WLADRON, AD2 PETE J. WESSINGER, AT2 DOUGLAS P. WIGGIN, AM2 JARED L. WIGGINS, AK2 MELISSA J. WILLETTE, AM3 GERADO AGUIRRE, AD3 MICHAEL R. ALLEN, AZ3 CYNTHIA BEAUCHAMPS, AT3 JOHN A. BRIDGEFORD, AM3 MICHELLE D. CHRISTIAN, AM3 EUGENE C. DEYO, AD3 MICHAEL S. DORROUGH, AO3 JIMMY M. GODWIN, AO3 JOANN B. GREEN, AM3 STEVE A. KELLEY, AT3 DAVID E. LACAZE, AM3 JOEL P. LAMPRICH, AM3 SHANNON M. LEONARD, AE3 ERIC L. McGAHA, AT3 JOSE R. MEDINA, AE3 TARA R. MITCHELL, AD3 JIMMY D. O'MARA, AZ3 TIMOTHY L. PECK, AD3 GABRIEL RAMIREZ, AZ3 CARLOS R. REYNOSO, YN3 KENDELL E. RICHARDSON, AM3 MICHAEL C. RICHARDSON, YN3 ANNETTE L. ROSS, YN3 STEPHEN D. SELMAN, AT3 SHANNON J. TAYLOR, AT3 SAMIRA P. TSCHUOR, AM3 SCHONN S. UNDERWOOD, AM3 JASON L. VIEMAN, ATAN THOMAS A. BOHL, AN STEVENS L. COLLINS, AN DAVID DeAnda, AMAN KORY L. GEESAMAN, ADAN MATTHEW T. HAAG, AN ERIC C. HEDSTROM, AOAN BOBBY L. HIX, AMEAN JAMES S. HUETTERMAN, AN LAWRENCE E. LAIRD, AMAN YAN L. LEVIN, AN RICHARD L. MATTHEWS, AN SHAWN P. McCLURE, ASAN BARK D. MILLER, AN FERNANDO PEREZ, AOAN MARCO V. PUMAYUGRA, AZAN VANNESSA REYES, AMAN ANDREW A. ROBERSON, AN ROBERT M. SCHLAICH, AOAN JAMIE L. SHIELDS, AOAN HARRY SYKES, AMAN BRYAN T. TRIGG, AOAN JOHN C. WEST, ADAN GREGG E. ZELLER, AMEAA JONATHAN A. JONE, AEAA DARYL W. LARSON, AEAA DERRICK R. WYNNS, SKSR CARLOS BELL, AMAR ADAM P. GEE. MATT WATTS (TECH REP)

NOTE – The list of above names came from the USS Theodore Roosevelt 2003 Cruise books Squadrons pages.

HUNTERS ACHIEVE EXCELLENCE

PASSING OF THE TORCH. Former Hunters and now Chiefs, Chief Duntley, Chief Joyner and Chief Ramirez present former Hunter and now Master Chief Marc Mayfield a Hunter plaque at his retirement ceremony. Former CO and now Admiral Sadler was also present at Master Mayfield's retirement ceremony.

Former Hunter Commanding Officer, now Admiral Chris "Tree" Sadler.

Former Hunter Commanding Officer, now Admiral Thomas W. Marratta.

Former Hunter Commanding Officer, now Admiral Doug "Woody" Beal.

Medal Of Honor

Melvin Morris

With Gary Sinise after his DFW Snowball Express Concert. A supporter of the book and its mission.

Gary Sinise with my Francine and I at the DFW Snowball Express event. Gary and his LT. Dan Band put on a 3 hour concert that night to show support for all our veterans. The Gary Sinise Foundation does so many great things for all our veterans.

Thank You Gary from ALL of us veterans whom you have helped out through your foundation.

WHAT IS A VETERAN

A "Veteran" – whether active duty, discharged, retired, or reserve – is someone who, at one point in his or her life, wrote a blank check made payable to "The United States of America," for an amount of "up to, and including his or her life."

ADDITIONAL COPIES OF THIS CAN BE PURCHASED THROUGH:

Amazon.com

AT THE FOLLOWING PRICES

ENJOY!

PAUL "PAULY" FREEMAN

Author

Paul "Pauly" Freeman is a native of Chicago, Illinois where he graduated from Weber High School. He enlisted as an airman 6 days after graduating High School in the U.S. Navy in 1984. He served on three different Aircraft Carriers as an Aviation Boatswain Mate Equipment and later as an Aviation Machinists Mate; USS Carl Vinson (CVN-70), USS John F. Kennedy (CV-67), the USS Theodore Roosevelt (CVN-71). He was an Aircraft Maintenance Chief during Operation Iraqi Freedom Air Strike Missions in 2003 onboard the USS Theodore Roosevelt (CVN-71). He also served in three squadrons; VA-304, VF-201, VFA-201. Paul retired in 2004 with the rank of Chief Petty Officer. Prior to Naval service retirement, he earned his Master's Degree in Aeronautical Science in Aerospace Operations from Embry Riddle Aeronautical University. He lives in Granbury Texas and is the father to one daughter, Taylor, two sons, Joseph and Andrew and is married to Francine. He still works in the Aviation Industry.

"ONCE A HUNTER ALWAYS A HUNTER"

Made in the USA
Middletown, DE
11 December 2024